INTRODUCTION

Welcome

What Makes This Book Different

The Real Secret: It Starts With How You Think

PART 1

THE FOUNDATIONS

CONTENTS

CONTENTS

CONTENTS

CLOSING CHAPTERS

WELCOME

"Change your conception of yourself and you will automatically change the world in which you live. Do not try to change people; they are only messengers telling you who you are. Revalue yourself and they will confirm the change."

— *Neville Goddard*

INTRODUCTION

Welcome to a journey that is not just about manifestation —
but about awakening.

I believe that true transformation begins from within. This
book is not just another guide on the Law of Attraction; it is
an invitation to remember who you really are: a powerful
creator, a magnetic being, a soul here to evolve.

The pages you're about to read will not just give you tools —
they will shift your way of thinking, feeling, and being.
Because attraction isn't something you "do". It's something
you are.

Whether you're new to this or have read dozens of books on
the subject, we invite you to open your heart, silence the
noise, and allow these words to activate a deeper knowing
within you.

Let this be the beginning of your **Magnetic Mind.**

INTRODUCTION

WHAT MAKES THIS BOOK DIFFERENT

You've probably heard about the Law of Attraction: "ask, believe, receive."

But no one tells you how to think — and that's the missing piece.

This book is different because it focuses not only on what to visualize or what to affirm, but on how to reshape the structure of your thinking.

Without understanding the mechanics of thought — how beliefs are formed, how emotions are triggered, and how subconscious programs run — all the affirmations in the world won't create lasting change.

We go deeper than just technique.

We explore how to build a mind that naturally attracts, by:

- Reprogramming subconscious patterns
- Feeling emotions before results arrive
- Releasing neediness and mental clutter
- Creating magnetic rituals that shift your inner state

You won't just learn what to do — you'll learn how to become.

THE REAL SECRET: IT STARTS WITH HOW YOU THINK

Your thoughts are not just words.

They are **vibrational commands** you send into the quantum field.

And here's the truth: You do not attract what you want You attract what you are thinking and feeling most consistently.

Most people try to manifest while still thinking in fear, doubt, or lack.

They wonder why nothing changes — not realizing their mental frequency is canceling their desires.

This book will teach you to think in **alignment with your highest vision.**

To think like the version of you who already has what they desire.

To think as a creator, not a victim.

Because once you master your inner world, **your outer reality has no choice but to shift.**

PART 1

WHAT IS THE LAW OF ATTRACTION, REALLY?

Beyond clichés: Energy, Vibration, and Focus

You've probably heard it before:
"Like attracts like."
"Ask, believe, receive."
"Thoughts become things."
But what does it actually mean?

Let's strip away the fluff and go to the essence:
The Law of Attraction is not about wishful thinking.

It is about vibration, alignment, and conscious focus.

◇ Everything is energy.

Modern science agrees with ancient wisdom:
At the most fundamental level, **everything is energy vibrating at different frequencies — including your thoughts, emotions, and intentions.**

Your mind is not just producing ideas; it is emitting a signal into the quantum field.

That signal becomes your point of attraction.
Just like a radio tunes into a specific frequency, the universe responds to the vibration you're constantly transmitting — not with words, but with energy patterns.

WHAT IS THE LAW OF ATTRACTION, REALLY?

◇ Your reality mirrors your inner state.

The Law of Attraction is not about forcing the universe to give you something.
It's about becoming a vibrational match to what you desire.
This means that:

- If you think thoughts of abundance and gratitude, you align with more abundance.
- If you dwell in fear, scarcity, or doubt, you magnetize more of that.
- If you act from love and wholeness, you naturally attract experiences that reflect that love and wholeness back to you.

◇ Focus is creative power.

Where you place your attention consistently, grows.
This is not just a spiritual idea — it's how your brain works.
The Reticular Activating System (RAS) in your brain filters your reality based on what you believe and focus on. This is why two people can walk into the same room and experience completely different things.

If you keep telling yourself, "Nothing ever works out for me," your brain (and your energy) will filter the world to confirm that.

WHAT IS THE LAW OF ATTRACTION, REALLY?

If you start thinking, "Everything is shifting in my favor," you'll begin to notice new opportunities, ideas, and synchronicities — because you're finally tuned into them.

✧ The Law of Attraction is always on.

This is important:
The Law of Attraction is not something you turn on when you do a meditation or say an affirmation.

It is always active — just like gravity.
You are always attracting based on your dominant vibration. This means you're either creating by default (unconsciously) or creating by design (intentionally).

This book will help you move from unconscious attraction to conscious creation.

✧ It's not about control — it's about coherence.

You don't have to control every thought. That's impossible. But you do have to create energetic coherence:
Where your thoughts, emotions, and actions are in harmony. When your mind is focused, your heart is open, and your body is aligned — you become a magnet for what you desire. This is the real Law of Attraction.

WHAT IS THE LAW OF ATTRACTION, REALLY?

Not just thinking positively, but thinking truthfully, feeling deeply, and choosing consciously — **until your inner state becomes more powerful than your outer circumstances.** And from that space, the extraordinary begins to unfold.

"Everything we call real is made of things that cannot be regarded as real."
Niels Bohr, quantum physicist and Nobel Prize winner

PART 2

THOUGHT IS CREATIVE ENERGY

Your Mind as a Frequency Emitter

Most people think thoughts are just private words in their heads.
But thoughts are not silent.
They are vibrational instructions — they carry energy, direction, and frequency.
Every thought you think sends out a wave. That wave interacts with other waves — in your body, in the field around you, and in the invisible web of energy we call "reality".

◇ Thoughts are electric. Emotions are magnetic.

Here is the formula:
Thoughts = electric signals.
Emotions = magnetic charge.
Together, they generate your personal vibrational field.
Think of your mind as a transmitter tower.

Every time you focus on a specific thought — especially with emotion — you're broadcasting a signal into the field of creation.
That signal either amplifies your desires or repels them, depending on the clarity, emotion, and repetition behind it.

PART 2

THOUGHT IS CREATIVE ENERGY

◇ Your mind is a builder.

A single thought might seem harmless. But repeated over time, thoughts become blueprints.
They build:

- **Your identity**
- **Your expectations**
- **Your emotional patterns**
- **And eventually... your circumstances**

You don't manifest what you think once.
You manifest what you think repeatedly, and most importantly, what you believe and feel to be true.
This is why fleeting affirmations don't work without inner alignment.

If your thoughts say, "I am abundant," but your emotional baseline says, "I don't feel safe," the signal becomes fragmented — and the universe responds to the dominant frequency, not the wishful one.

PART 2

THOUGHT IS CREATIVE ENERGY

◇ The danger of unconscious thinking

Most people are thinking the same 90% of thoughts every single day.

And most of them are unconscious, reactive, and rooted in the past. This is why many people stay stuck:
They're broadcasting yesterday's fears, old limitations, and inherited beliefs — while hoping for a new future.

Until you learn to become aware of your thoughts and consciously redirect them, your mind will keep recreating the same loops.

You can't build a new life with the same thoughts that created the old one.

THOUGHT IS CREATIVE ENERGY

✧ Thoughts set direction. Emotions give them power.

If thought is the arrow, then emotion is the bow.
The stronger the emotion, the further your intention flies.
This is why empty thoughts don't manifest.

Only thoughts that are charged with emotional energy create real impact in the field.
This is also why fear manifests powerfully:
Because it is charged, focused, and often repeated.

Your job is to apply that same energetic commitment to your highest vision — not your worst fears.

✧ You are always creating — with every thought.

There is no pause button.
The question is not, "Am I creating?"
The real question is:
"Am I creating what I actually want?"

To shift your life, you must start thinking as the **future version of yourself** — the one who already lives the reality you desire.

THOUGHT IS CREATIVE ENERGY

Not from your wounds.
Not from your worries.
But from the version of you who has already arrived.
That is when thought becomes creation.

🔑 Key Takeaways:

- Thoughts are not passive. They emit frequency.
- Emotions magnetize thoughts and make them manifest.
- Repetition + feeling = reprogramming.
- You are the architect of your reality — thought by thought.
- Change your thoughts, and you change your energy. Change your energy, and you change your life.

"You must learn a new way to think before you can master a new way to be."
— Marianne Williamson

THE MIND–EMOTION LOOP

How Thoughts Create Emotions, and Emotions Reinforce Thoughts

You don't just think your way into a new life — you feel your way into it.
But here's the key:
Your thoughts create your emotions,
and your emotions feed back into your thoughts.
This creates a loop — and depending on your awareness, that loop can either trap you...
or set you free.

◇ **Every thought triggers a chemical response.**

Let's look at the science.
When you think a thought — for example, "I'm not good enough" — your brain sends signals to your body that trigger emotional chemicals: cortisol, adrenaline, or sadness-inducing neuropeptides.
Those chemicals don't just vanish.
They get stored in your nervous system, your posture, your energy field.

THE MIND–EMOTION LOOP

Your body starts feeling what the mind is saying — and then the body sends signals back to the mind saying,
"This is how we feel. Keep thinking that way."
The loop is complete.

Thought → Emotion → Body → More Thoughts → Stronger Emotion.

◇ Emotion makes thought real.

A thought without emotion is just noise.
But when emotion joins the thought — it becomes a command.

That's why people struggle with affirmations like "I am confident" — **if it's not backed by a real feeling, the subconscious mind rejects it.**

On the other hand, a deeply felt emotion (positive or negative) burns the thought into your system, like data onto a hard drive.

If you think "I always fail" while feeling frustrated and hopeless, you're reinforcing a loop that will become your identity — and soon, your reality.

PART 3

THE MIND–EMOTION LOOP

◇ **Most people live in emotional memory, not emotional choice.**

Here's a truth no one talks about:
Most of what you feel each day isn't actually based on the present.
It's a replay of old thoughts, past wounds, and emotional conditioning.
You're not sad because of today —
You're sad because your mind is replaying a narrative you haven't stopped believing.
And until you interrupt that loop, your system will keep predicting the past, not creating the future.

◇ **The body becomes addicted to emotion.**

Yes — you can become addicted to anger.
To sadness.
To fear.
Why? Because your body gets used to the chemical state those emotions create.
So even when your mind wants something new, your body pulls you back into what's familiar.
That's why change often feels uncomfortable — because you're breaking emotional patterns the body thinks are "safe".

THE MIND–EMOTION LOOP

To rewire your vibration, you must feel differently long enough for the body to accept a new baseline.

◇ The key is emotional mastery — not emotional suppression.

You don't manifest by pretending to be happy all the time. You manifest by becoming emotionally conscious — by noticing what you feel, understanding where it comes from, and choosing new emotions on purpose.

That's where real power begins.

◇ Break the loop. Create a new one.

Here's the formula for a magnetic loop:
Thought → Emotion → Body → Feedback → Result

You no longer wait to feel good because something good happened.
You feel good to attract something good.
And in doing so, you break free from the loop of reaction...
and step into the loop of creation.

PART 3

THE MIND–EMOTION LOOP

🔑 Key Takeaways:

- Thoughts and emotions form a feedback loop — one that can trap or liberate you.
- Emotion gives power to thought. Feeling = fuel.
- Most emotions are habits — not truth.
- You can train your body to feel differently, and shift your vibration permanently.
- Choose to feel in alignment with your future, not your past.

"Whether you think you can, or you think you can't — you're right." Henry Ford

THE SCIENCE BEHIND ATTRACTION

Quantum Fields, Brain Wiring & the Invisible Mechanics of Reality

The Law of Attraction is not just a spiritual idea.
It has roots in neuroscience, biology, and even quantum physics.
When you understand the mechanics behind it, it stops feeling "woo-woo" and starts feeling inevitable.
You are not just thinking — you are broadcasting, rewiring, and collapsing possibilities into reality.

◇ Your brain is plastic — and programmable.

The brain is not static. It changes based on what you repeatedly think and feel.
This is called neuroplasticity.
Every time you think a thought, you fire a neural pathway.
The more you repeat that thought, the stronger the pathway becomes.
Eventually, that thought becomes automatic — a belief.
That's how identity forms. Not from truth — but from repetition. The good news?

PART 4

THE SCIENCE BEHIND ATTRACTION

You can reprogram your brain by choosing new thoughts, pairing them with emotion, and practicing daily focus. Affirmations, visualizations, and journaling aren't magic. They are mental training tools that reshape your brain's structure.

◇ Your subconscious runs the show.

Up to 95% of your actions are driven by your subconscious mind. That includes your habits, emotional responses, and even your sense of self-worth.

The subconscious doesn't understand logic — it speaks emotion, repetition, and imagery.

That's why visualizing with feeling works better than overthinking your goals.

When you align your subconscious programming with your desires, your entire system works in harmony — and manifestation becomes natural.

THE SCIENCE BEHIND ATTRACTION

◇ The Reticular Activating System (RAS)

Imagine you buy a red car — and suddenly, you see red cars everywhere.
That's not the universe sending signs. That's your Reticular Activating System doing its job.
The RAS is a filter in your brain that selects what information is relevant.

It shows you what matches your dominant beliefs and focus.
So if you constantly think, "I'm not enough", the RAS highlights proof of rejection, failure, and scarcity.
If you start thinking, "I am supported and capable," it will highlight proof of that instead. Your brain literally rearranges your perception of reality based on what you believe.

◇ The quantum field responds to intention.

At the subatomic level, reality behaves differently than in the physical world.
In quantum physics, particles exist as probabilities — until they're observed.
This means that your attention collapses potential into form.
Observation = creation.

THE SCIENCE BEHIND ATTRACTION

When you focus your thoughts and emotions on a specific intention, you're sending information into the field — and aligning with one possible timeline over another.
You are not pulling things "to you."

You are tuning your vibration to an already-existing possibility — and letting it collapse into your timeline.

◇ Coherence is the key.

Coherence means your heart, brain, and body are in harmony.
In this state, your electromagnetic field becomes stronger, clearer, and more attractive.
HeartMath research shows that when people enter a state of heart coherence (gratitude, love, compassion), they:

- **Improve immune function**
- **Shift brainwave patterns**
- **Enhance intuition**
- **Affect the energy field around them up to several feet**

This isn't imagination.

It's biology — aligned with vibration.

PART 4

THE SCIENCE BEHIND ATTRACTION

◇ You are a field, not just a body.

Your body is surrounded by an electromagnetic field, created
by your heart and brain.
That field changes based on your thoughts and emotions —
and interacts with the energy fields of others.

**When you think thoughts that are coherent, high-
frequency, and emotionally charged, your field expands
and becomes magnetic.**

Others feel it.
Opportunities align.
Reality responds.

🔑 Key Takeaways:

- Your brain is rewired by repetition, emotion, and belief.
- Your subconscious controls most of your attraction
  power.
- The RAS filters your world based on what you expect.
- Quantum physics confirms: focused attention creates
  reality.
- You are a field of energy — not just a thinker, but a
  transmitter.

THE SCIENCE BEHIND ATTRACTION

"Until you make the unconscious conscious, it will direct your life and you will call it fate."
— Carl Jung

PART 5

WHY MOST PEOPLE FAIL

Resistance, Subconscious Sabotage, and Lack of Emotional Alignment

Let's be honest.
Most people know about the Law of Attraction...
but they don't actually get results.
They visualize.
They say affirmations.
They watch all the right videos.
And yet — nothing seems to change.
Why?
Because they're trying to manifest from a misaligned inner state.
In this chapter, we'll explore the real reasons behind failed manifestations — and how to finally break free.

◇ 1. They're thinking from lack.
Wanting something is not the same as attracting it.
In fact, **many people are wanting from a place of absence**.
They say things like:

- "I want money" — but feel poor.
- "I want love" — but feel unworthy.
- "I want peace" — but feel overwhelmed.

WHY MOST PEOPLE FAIL

Here's the trap:
You attract not what you want,
but what you feel when your desire is filled with desperation,
you're sending the signal:
"I don't have it."
And the universe responds accordingly.

◇ 2. They skip emotional alignment.

The universe doesn't respond to words. It responds to emotion + vibration.
You can say "I am abundant" 100 times a day,
but if you feel anxious, ashamed, or doubtful — **your emotional signal will cancel the words.**

Most people try to change their reality with mental effort,
but don't do the deeper work of feeling different first.
Emotional alignment isn't optional. It's the engine of attraction.

WHY MOST PEOPLE FAIL

◇ 3. Their subconscious programming is in conflict.

Remember: 95% of your life is driven by subconscious patterns.
You might consciously want success...
but if your subconscious believes that success = stress, rejection, or unworthiness,
it will block the path. Every time.
This is why self-sabotage happens.
It's not weakness. It's protection — based on outdated beliefs.
Until you reprogram your subconscious (through repetition, imagery, journaling, and somatic awareness), it will always override your conscious desires.

◇ 4. They force instead of allowing.

Manifestation isn't about control.
It's about alignment, then allowing.
But many people get impatient. They start pushing, overthinking, chasing outcomes.
This energy of force creates resistance — and resistance slows everything down.
The more you try to control how and when it happens,
the more you block the flow of divine timing and synchronicity.

PART 5

WHY MOST PEOPLE FAIL

The paradox: Things arrive faster when you're no longer desperate for them.

✧ 5. They don't stay consistent.

One vision. Ten doubts.
That's how most people operate.
They feel inspired in the morning, aligned for an hour...
and then spend the rest of the day worrying, reacting, scrolling.
Manifestation isn't about doing it perfectly.
It's about becoming stable in your vibration — especially when life gets chaotic.
That's why daily rituals (like journaling, meditation, and mental focus) are essential.
They help you return to your magnetic state, over and over again — until it becomes who you are.

✧ 6. They confuse signs with outcomes.

A common mistake:
People expect instant results — and when they don't see them, they get discouraged.
But attraction works like nature. You plant, you nurture, and then you harvest — not in the same moment.
Often, the universe sends small signs first:
opportunities, ideas, encounters, energy shifts.

WHY MOST PEOPLE FAIL

If you ignore these signs because they're "not big enough," you miss the proof that it's already working.

🔑 Key Takeaways:

- You can't manifest from fear, need, or doubt — even if your words are "positive".
- The subconscious mind must be reprogrammed, not bypassed.
- Alignment is more powerful than effort.
- Emotion is the fuel. Repetition is the key. Trust is the flow.
- The journey of attraction is the journey of becoming.

"Every action you take is a vote for the type of person you wish to become."
— James Clear

HOW A THOUGHT BECOMES A THING

The Invisible Chain: Thought → Feeling → Vibration → Action → Manifestation

Have you ever wondered how a simple thought could possibly create a physical reality?
It sounds magical — but there's a real, consistent chain of creation behind it.
And once you understand that chain, you can consciously direct it.
You stop reacting... and start creating.
Let's break it down step by step.

◇ 1. Thought: The Seed

Everything starts with a thought.
But not just any thought — a focused, intentional one.
Like a seed planted in the soil, a thought holds the blueprint of a future reality.
Examples:

- "I want to live by the ocean."
- "I feel called to build something of my own."
- "I know I'm meant for more."

Thought is the first spark — the signal sent into the quantum field. But a seed alone doesn't grow. It needs emotional energy to activate it.

HOW A THOUGHT
BECOMES A THING

✧ 2. Feeling: The Water

Emotion is what gives a thought life.
Without feeling, a thought stays in the mind. With feeling, it enters the energetic field.
Think of it this way:
Thoughts send the signal. Emotions attract the experience.
When you feel something as if it's already real, your nervous system starts to rewire, your field begins to shift, and your vibration changes.
The universe doesn't respond to what you want.
It responds to what you are — and feeling is how you become it.

✧ 3. Vibration: The Frequency

Once a thought is emotionally charged, it becomes a vibrational signature.
This frequency is what the universe "reads."
Every thought-emotion pair broadcasts a unique energetic code.

HOW A THOUGHT BECOMES A THING

Think of it like tuning a radio station:

- **Gratitude, trust, love = high frequency**
- **Fear, doubt, frustration = low frequency**

You attract what matches your station — not what you're trying to force.
Change the frequency, and you change the type of experience that flows into your life.

◇ 4. Action: The Bridge

Aligned action is where most people get it wrong — they either do nothing and "wait," or they do too much from a state of stress.
Manifestation is not about hustle.
It's about inspired movement — taking steps from a place of trust, not desperation.
When your thoughts, emotions, and vibration are aligned, you'll receive intuitive nudges:
calls to act, to speak, to build, to shift.
These are not coincidences. They are the bridges your higher self is building.
You don't manifest by doing nothing.
You manifest by becoming magnetic — and then responding to the openings that appear.

PART 6

HOW A THOUGHT
BECOMES A THING

✧ 5. Manifestation: The Fruit

When thought, emotion, vibration, and action are in
harmony, manifestation becomes inevitable.
It may not happen overnight — but it will happen.
Why?
Because you've shifted from wanting to embodying.
From wishing to knowing.
And from force to flow.
The outcome becomes a natural extension of who you are.
That's when the "thing" shows up — the opportunity, the
person, the shift, the abundance.

✧ It's not magic. It's mastery.

This process isn't mystical. It's repeatable.
Like a recipe.
But here's the catch:
You must stay consistent with your inner state before.
If you wait to feel successful after success shows up, you
delay the process.

**If you choose to feel successful now, you align your entire
system to let it in.**

That's how a thought becomes a thing.

PART 6

HOW A THOUGHT BECOMES A THING

■ Summary: The Manifestation Chain

1. Thought → sets the intention
2. Emotion → activates the frequency
3. Vibration → broadcasts the energy
4. Aligned Action → builds the path
5. Manifestation → reality shifts to match your state

🔑 Key Takeaways:

- A thought without emotion is powerless.
- Emotion fuels vibration — and vibration attracts.
- Inspired action connects your inner world to the physical one.
- Manifestation is not magic — it's the result of internal alignment.
- You don't wait to believe it's possible. You believe, and then it becomes possible.

"You begin to fly when you let go of self-limiting beliefs and allow your mind and aspirations to rise to greater heights."
— Brian Tracy

THE TRUTH ABOUT BELIEFS

Core Beliefs and Identity Programming

Here's a radical truth:
You don't attract what you want.
You attract what you believe you.
This is why you can visualize, affirm, and meditate...
and still feel stuck.
Because beneath the surface, your beliefs may be sending out
a completely different signal.
Let's dive into what beliefs are, how they form, and how to
finally reprogram the ones that block your power.

◇ What is a belief?

A belief is simply a thought you've repeated enough times —
often with emotion — until it feels like truth.
It becomes part of your identity.
Not because it's objectively true...
but because your mind and body got used to it.
Belief = Familiar thought + Emotional charge + Repetition

THE TRUTH ABOUT BELIEFS

Once installed, beliefs operate silently in the background. They shape how you see yourself, others, and what's possible. They are the lens through which you interpret life — and they determine what your subconscious allows or rejects.

◇ Beliefs are stronger than intentions.

You may want to be wealthy, but if you believe money is dangerous or that you don't deserve it — you'll unconsciously block it.

You may want love, but if you believe people can't be trusted — you'll sabotage relationships.

You may want freedom, but if you believe it requires sacrifice or pain — you'll stay in limitation.

Beliefs always win over desires — unless you update the belief system.

THE TRUTH ABOUT BELIEFS

◇ Where do beliefs come from?

Most of your core beliefs were formed between the ages of 0 and 7.
At that age, your brain was in a theta state — like a sponge, absorbing everything as truth.
You didn't have filters. You became whatever your environment taught you.
Sources of your beliefs include:

- **Family and childhood experiences**
- **Cultural and religious conditioning**
- **School, authority figures, and media**
- **Repeated emotional events (especially trauma)**

These early beliefs became the operating system of your mind.

And unless you update that system consciously, you'll keep repeating the same patterns — even if your adult self wants different results.

THE TRUTH ABOUT BELIEFS

◇ Your identity is a belief structure.

We all walk around with invisible "I am" statements that define us:

- "I am not enough."
- "I am not creative."
- "I am bad with money."
- "I am too much."
- "I am not lovable."
- "I am not safe."

These are not facts — they are beliefs.
And they create your energetic signature.
If you want to attract a different reality, you must start believing a different version of you.

◇ Beliefs create filters and limits.

Once a belief is in place, your mind will do two things:

1. **Look for evidence that confirms it**
2. **Reject anything that contradicts it**

This is called confirmation bias, and it's incredibly powerful. If you believe people can't be trusted, your brain will ignore kind acts and focus only on betrayals.

THE TRUTH ABOUT BELIEFS

If you believe success is hard, you won't notice opportunities that look "too easy".
Your beliefs shape your perception, and perception becomes your reality.

◇ Beliefs can be rewritten.

Here's the best part:
Beliefs are not fixed.
They can be transformed through:

- Repetition of new thoughts
- Emotional imprinting (feeling the new belief as true)
- Visualizing from the new identity
- Journaling to challenge and replace old programs
- Embodiment — acting "as if" the new belief were already real

You don't need to be perfect.
You just need to be consistent.

THE TRUTH ABOUT BELIEFS

■ From limiting to liberating:

Let's take an example.
Old Belief: "I'm not good enough to be seen."

➡ Creates fear of visibility, rejection, and self-sabotage.
New Belief: "My voice is valuable, and the world is ready for me."
➡ Creates courage, creativity, and aligned visibility.
That one shift can change everything — from the relationships you attract to the income you receive.

🔑 Key Takeaways:

- Beliefs are not truths — they are conditioned thoughts.
- Your current identity is a belief system in disguise.
- What you believe about yourself becomes the limit of what you can receive.
- You can rewire any belief through repetition, feeling, and action.
- When your beliefs change, your vibration — and your life — transform.

"Your word is your wand. The words you speak create your own destiny."
— Florence Scovel Shinn

CLEANING YOUR MENTAL FIELD

Releasing Limiting Thoughts and Stories

Imagine trying to tune into a specific radio frequency — but there's static, noise, and five other stations playing at once. That's what happens when you try to manifest with a cluttered mind.

Your intentions are unclear. Your energy is divided. Your signal gets scrambled. **If you want to become magnetic, you need to clean your mental field** — just like you'd clear a garden before planting new seeds. Let's learn how.

⬦ Your mental field is your vibrational space.

Every thought you think lives somewhere in your energy field.
And like dust on a mirror, old thoughts — especially fear-based or repetitive ones — distort your reflection.
This mental noise becomes:

- **Inner conflict**
- **Self-doubt**
- **Confusion**
- **Emotional fatigue**
- **A magnet for chaos**

CLEANING YOUR MENTAL FIELD

Your outer life becomes cluttered because your inner space is full of old patterns.

◇ Step 1: Identify your dominant thought patterns.

The first step to clearing is awareness.
You can't release what you haven't noticed.
Ask yourself:

- What thoughts do I think every day without even realizing it?
- Are these thoughts empowering or draining?
- Where do they come from — my truth, or someone else's fear?

You'll often find stories like:

- "This is too good to be true."
- "It never works for me."
- "If I try, I'll fail."
- "Better play small than be hurt."

These are not truths. They are programmed narratives — and they can be rewritten.

CLEANING YOUR MENTAL FIELD

◇ Step 2: Declutter your mental environment.

Your mind doesn't operate in a vacuum.
Your inputs matter.

Start decluttering:

- Who you listen to — silence toxic voices and unconscious negativity.
- What you consume — replace news, gossip, and overstimulation with nourishing content.
- How you speak — stop reinforcing limitation through casual language. ("I'm so tired of this," "Nothing works," "Just my luck.")

Your mind is fertile ground.
Be careful what you allow to grow there.

CLEANING YOUR MENTAL FIELD

✧ Step 3: Interrupt the loop.

When a limiting thought arises, don't fight it — observe it. Say to yourself:

"This is just an old signal. It's not who I am."
Then replace it with a higher-frequency thought.

Example:

- Old: "Nothing ever changes."
- New: "Everything is shifting in my favor."

You're not lying to yourself.
You're retraining your perception — and your energy will begin to follow.

CLEANING YOUR MENTAL FIELD

◇ Step 4: Energetic hygiene is mental hygiene.

Just like you brush your teeth daily, you must clear your mental energy regularly.

Here are simple practices that help:

- Meditation – to quiet inner noise and reset your vibration
- Journaling – to release looping thoughts and process emotion
- Breathwork – to move stagnant energy
- Nature walks – to reset your nervous system
- Visualization – to clean your mental screen and replace it with clarity

You don't need to do all of them together. Just start with one practice and stay consistent for a period of time.

CLEANING YOUR MENTAL FIELD

✧ You can't attract clearly from a cluttered mind.

Trying to manifest from mental chaos is like shouting into a storm — the message gets lost.
When your inner world is quiet, clean, and clear, the signal you send becomes coherent — and the universe hears you instantly.

■ Summary Process: Cleaning Your Mind

1. Awareness – Notice your most common thought patterns
2. Declutter – Remove inputs and influences that drain your energy
3. Interrupt – Gently stop loops with conscious replacement
4. Reset – Use daily practices to clear and recharge your mind
5. Align – Think only from the version of you who already has what you want

CLEANING YOUR MENTAL FIELD

🔑 Key Takeaways:

- Your mind is a vibrational field — not a container of thoughts.
- Mental clutter sends mixed signals and weakens manifestation.
- Cleaning your field means clearing people, media, language, and emotion.
- The clearer your mind, the faster your desires flow.
- Your inner clarity becomes your outer magnetism.

"Your thoughts are not contained in your head — they are broadcast into the field. Clean your mind, and you clean the signal you're sending to the universe."
— Bruce H. Lipton

THE LANGUAGE OF THE SUBCONSCIOUS

Symbols, Repetition, Imagery, and Emotion

Your subconscious mind doesn't speak in words.

It speaks in images, feelings, symbols, and repetition.

That's why logic rarely creates transformation — but a single, vivid experience can change your life.
To reprogram your subconscious and activate deep manifestation, you must learn to communicate in its native language.

◇ The subconscious learns through repetition.

What you repeat, you become.
This isn't metaphor — it's neurological programming.
The subconscious mind doesn't judge whether something is good or bad, true or false.
It simply absorbs what it sees, hears, and feels most often.

Repetition + Emotion = Installation

This is why affirmations only work when you use them consistently and feel them deeply.
A belief is not formed by saying something once — it's formed by hearing it over and over, especially in emotional states.

THE LANGUAGE OF THE SUBCONSCIOUS

◇ Emotion is the gateway.

Emotion is what burns information into the subconscious.
That's why trauma creates such strong beliefs — not because
the story was true, but because the emotional intensity
locked it in.
**To reprogram a belief, you must pair a new message with
strong feeling: joy, gratitude, empowerment, expansion.**

That emotional charge opens the "gate" to your subconscious
— and lets the new belief in.

◇ The mind thinks in pictures.

Try this: don't think of a pink elephant.
What happened? You saw it — instantly.
Your subconscious doesn't process negatives, or abstract
sentences. It processes images.
That's why visualization is so powerful:
When you imagine something vividly and emotionally, your
subconscious can't tell the difference between "real" and
"imagined."
To the mind, it's all now.
And what you live in your inner world becomes magnetic in
the outer world.

THE LANGUAGE OF THE SUBCONSCIOUS

◇ Symbols are shortcuts to deep meaning.

Throughout history, symbols have held immense power:
the cross, the lotus, the ouroboros, the eye, the spiral.
That's because the subconscious stores meaning in symbolic form.
A single image can unlock a deep emotional state faster than a paragraph.

Use this to your advantage:

- **Create a vision board filled with images that represent the feeling of your future.**
- **Use objects as energetic anchors (crystals, totems, jewelry with intention).**
- **Draw or sketch what your new identity "looks" like to your inner mind.**

Symbols bypass the analytical brain — and speak directly to your deeper self.

PART 9

THE LANGUAGE OF THE SUBCONSCIOUS

◇ Stories rewire identity.

The subconscious loves narratives.
This is why we are so moved by movies, books, and mythologies — they speak in archetypes.
To shift your subconscious, tell a new story:

- "I used to be stuck, but now I'm rising."
- "I am the one who breaks the cycle."
- "I am chosen, capable, guided."

Your subconscious doesn't need data — it needs a hero's journey to follow.
Make yourself the hero.
Let your life become the story your subconscious believes in.

◇ Protect your subconscious input.

Your subconscious is always listening — especially when your mind is relaxed.
Be intentional with what you feed it:

- **The first and last 20 minutes of your day are prime programming time.**
- **Avoid consuming fear-based media before sleep.**
- **Use sleep meditations, audio affirmations, or journaling at night to rewire.**

THE LANGUAGE OF THE SUBCONSCIOUS

Whatever you let in just before sleep sinks deepest.

🔑 Key Takeaways:

- The subconscious speaks in imagery, emotion, repetition, and symbolism.
- To reprogram it, use emotional affirmations, visualizations, and symbolic anchors.
- Stories are powerful rewriters of identity — choose your narrative.
- Protect your inputs. Every thought and image matters.
- Speak to your subconscious in the language it understands — and it will reshape your life.

"The conscious mind may be the goal setter, but the subconscious mind is the goal getter."
— Denis Waitley

REWIRING THE MIND FOR MAGNETIC POWER

Visualization, Affirmations, and Identity-Shifting

Now that you understand how the subconscious works, it's time to go deeper:
into the practical tools that allow you to reprogram your mind, upgrade your frequency, and become truly magnetic. This isn't about "thinking positive."
It's about installing a new operating system — one that is aligned with the future you want to attract.

✧ Repetition builds identity.

Your brain is designed to adapt.
Whatever you think, feel, and repeat becomes your mental default.
This means that with conscious repetition, you can teach your brain to:

- Expect good things
- Feel safe receiving
- Recognize aligned opportunities
- Think like your future self

The more you repeat thoughts aligned with your vision — with emotion — the faster they become automatic programs.

PART 10

REWIRING THE MIND FOR MAGNETIC POWER

◇ Visualization creates new neural maps.

When you vividly imagine a scenario, your brain fires the same neurons as if you were actually living it.
This is called neuroplastic rehearsal — and it's how athletes, performers, and visionaries prime themselves for success.
Visualization is most powerful when:

- You see the scene through your own eyes
- You include as many senses as possible
- You add emotion: joy, gratitude, love, power
- You practice daily, even for just 5 minutes

The key is consistency. The more real it feels inside, the faster it shows up outside.

◇ Affirmations shift self-image.

Affirmations are not magic words — they are identity scripts. You're not just repeating nice phrases. You're telling your brain: "This is who I am now." But they only work if:

- You believe they are possible (even just 5%)
- You say them with feeling, not flatly
- You repeat them often, especially in relaxed states
- You pair them with action and evidence

REWIRING THE MIND FOR MAGNETIC POWER

Example:
"I am becoming more confident every day."
Is more effective than:
"I am the most powerful person alive" (if you don't believe it at all).
The subconscious accepts what is emotionally believable and consistently heard.

◇ Act "as if" — not to fake it, but to feel it.

Identity shifting happens when your actions reflect the version of you you're becoming.
Ask yourself:

- How would the "magnetic me" walk into a room?
- What would they say no to?
- What thoughts would they think in this moment?
- What choices would they make today?

Living "as if" rewires the brain through embodiment.
You're not faking it. You're training your nervous system to feel safe in the new version of you.
And when your identity shifts, your entire energetic signature changes.

REWIRING THE MIND FOR MAGNETIC POWER

◇ Combine tools for maximum power.

You don't need 100 techniques. You need 3–4 practices done consistently.

A powerful daily rewiring sequence:

1. Morning visualization — step into your future self
2. Written affirmations — "I am" statements + gratitude
3. Voice repetition — record your affirmations, listen while walking
4. Aligned action — one bold move that reflects your new identity

The mind changes through feeling + repetition + movement. The more ways you engage the process, the faster it locks in.

PART 10

REWIRING THE MIND
FOR MAGNETIC POWER

🔑 **Key Takeaways:**

- Your brain is programmable — repetition and emotion are the code.
- Visualization builds internal maps for success.
- Affirmations shift identity when done with belief and consistency.
- Acting "as if" trains your nervous system to accept the new you.
- Combine tools into a daily ritual to rewire your magnetic mind.

"Whatever we plant in our subconscious mind and nourish with repetition and emotion will one day become a reality."
— Earl Nightingale

PART 11

THE ROLE OF CLARITY AND FOCUS

Why Vague Desires Repel and Clear Intentions Attract

The universe doesn't respond to confusion.
It responds to clarity — clear energy, clear thoughts, clear direction.
Many people say they want "a better life," "more abundance," or "true love"...
but those are vague desires. And vagueness sends a weak, scattered signal.
To become magnetic, your desires must become precise, embodied, and emotionally defined.

◇ **Vague goals = vague results.**

When your mind is unclear, your vibration is unstable.
You attract random situations, mixed signals, or... nothing at all. If you walk into a restaurant and say, "I want food," the waiter won't know what to bring.
But if you say, "I want the warm quinoa bowl with roasted vegetables and lemon dressing,"
your request is fulfilled with ease.
The same applies to the universe.
Be specific.

THE ROLE OF CLARITY AND FOCUS

✧ Clarity sharpens your vibration.

A clear intention activates multiple systems at once:

- **Your conscious focus**
- **Your subconscious direction**
- **Your emotional alignment**
- **Your energetic field**

It becomes a laser beam, not a scattered light.
When you know what you want, why you want it, and how it will feel — you become magnetic.

✧ Focus is energetic commitment.

Where you place your attention, energy flows.
And where your energy flows, reality grows.
Every time you switch goals, question yourself, or second-guess your desires,
you dilute the signal.
Instead, choose one clear desire and commit to it.
Let it become a home frequency — something you return to daily.

Focused energy creates momentum.
And momentum builds manifestation.

PART 11

THE ROLE OF CLARITY
AND FOCUS

◇ The mind loves to wander — train it to return.

Your job is not to be perfect.
Your job is to return to clarity every time you drift.
Mental discipline is spiritual power.
Use tools to stay focused:

- **Write your vision every morning**
- **Create a mantra you repeat throughout the day**
- **Use visual anchors in your environment**
- **Set intentions before sleep**

Don't wait to "feel ready."
Clarity is a decision, not a mood.

◇ Know the essence, not just the form.

Being clear doesn't mean controlling the exact form of your
desire.
It means knowing the feeling, quality, and impact of what
you want.
Example:
"I want to feel deeply connected, respected, and alive in my
relationship."

THE ROLE OF CLARITY AND FOCUS

is more magnetic than:
"I want a partner who is 6'2, dark-haired, and plays guitar."
Let the essence guide the form.
The universe often delivers something even better than what you imagined.

🔑 Key Takeaways:

- Vague desires confuse your mind and your field.
- Clarity creates coherence — and coherence attracts.
- Focused energy is more powerful than scattered action.
- Return to your intention daily until it becomes your baseline.
- Feel the essence, and let the form unfold through aligned resonance.

"Clarity precedes success."
— Robin Sharma

EMOTION: THE MAGNET OF MANIFESTATION

Matching Your Vibration to What You Want

If thought is the signal you send...
emotion is the magnet that pulls experiences to you.
You don't manifest what you think — **you manifest what you feel to be real.**
This is why feeling good isn't just nice — it's necessary.
Your emotional state determines your vibrational frequency, and that frequency attracts the people, opportunities, and situations that match it.

✧ Emotion = Energy in motion.

Every emotion you feel sends out a wave.
That wave carries information into the quantum field — and shapes what comes back.

High-frequency emotions:

- Love
- Gratitude
- Joy
- Trust
- Excitement

EMOTION: THE MAGNET OF MANIFESTATION

Low-frequency emotions:

- Fear
- Shame
- Anger
- Guilt
- Hopelessness

Neither is "wrong" — but your dominant emotional tone becomes your attraction point.

◇ Feeling is faster than thinking.

You can try to "think positive" all day,
but if you're vibrating in anxiety, your field is still broadcasting fear.
Emotion is instant frequency.
One moment of deep gratitude can shift your entire signal more than hours of mental effort.
The fastest way to change your vibration is to change how you feel — now.

EMOTION: THE MAGNET OF MANIFESTATION

✧ Feel it before you see it.

Most people wait for life to give them a reason to feel good.
But the masters — the magnetic ones — **choose to feel good in advance.**
This is the paradox:
You don't feel happy because
You manifest something because
Feel abundance, and abundance moves toward you.
Feel love, and love recognizes you.
Feel peace, and life reorganizes itself to reflect that.

✧ Anchor emotions into your body.

Don't just feel in your head.
Drop the emotion into your body:

- **Smile**
- **Open your chest**
- **Breathe deeply**
- **Move like the version of you who already has it**

Let the emotion become physical — and your vibration becomes stable.

EMOTION: THE MAGNET OF MANIFESTATION

✧ Emotional rehearsal builds magnetism.

Every day, take 3 minutes to feel the emotional state of your desired reality.
Not the thing — the feeling behind the thing.
Examples:

- Don't just visualize money — feel freedom, expansion, and generosity
- Don't just visualize love — feel safety, joy, connection
- Don't just visualize success — feel confidence, clarity, celebration

This emotional practice trains your nervous system to believe: **"It's already happening."**

And when your system believes it — your world catches up.

EMOTION: THE MAGNET OF MANIFESTATION

🔑 Key Takeaways:

- Emotion is your true vibration — not thought alone.
- High-frequency emotions magnetize aligned outcomes.
- Feel your future now to attract it faster.
- Anchor emotion in the body for lasting impact.
- Practice emotional alignment daily — even 3 minutes is enough.

"Emotion is the force of life. It shapes decisions, creates destiny, and fuels every action we take."
— Tony Robbins

HOW TO GENERATE EMOTIONS ON-DEMAND

Memory, Embodiment, and Sensory Hacking

To manifest powerfully, you must learn to feel first — even before there's a reason.
But how do you feel abundance when you're broke?
How do you feel love when you're alone?
The secret is simple:
Emotion is not a reaction.
Emotion is a skill.
Let's explore how to generate elevated emotions on command, using the tools already inside you.

◇ Memory is a portal.

Your brain doesn't distinguish between real and imagined events — or between past and present.
This means you can use positive memories to generate emotion now.

Try this:

- Recall a moment of deep joy, love, peace, or confidence
- Close your eyes and relive it in full detail
- Feel what your body felt then — breathe it in
- Let that emotion flood your nervous system

HOW TO GENERATE EMOTIONS ON-DEMAND

Now — associate that emotion with your current desire. You've just anchored your future to a proven emotional frequency.

✧ Embodiment creates immediate shifts.

You don't always need thoughts to feel.
Your body posture and movement can trigger emotion directly.

Try this:

- Stand tall, shoulders back, heart open
- Breathe deeply
- Smile (even slightly)
- Walk like someone who is powerful and at peace

You're now embodying a new signal.
The body leads — and the mind follows.
Use music, movement, dance, or breathwork to access elevated states without needing a reason.

PART 13

HOW TO GENERATE EMOTIONS ON-DEMAND

✧ Use sensory hacking.

The fastest way to change how you feel is to change what your senses are experiencing.
This includes:

- Sound: Play music that lifts or empowers you
- Smell: Use essential oils or scents linked to calm and joy
- Sight: Look at images that evoke beauty, nature, success
- Touch: Wear clothes that make you feel abundant and alive
- Taste: Eat something consciously, with gratitude and presence

You're training your nervous system to feel good — here and now. That feeling becomes your new emotional baseline.

✧ Assign emotions to daily anchors.

Use objects, moments, or habits as emotional triggers.
Examples:

- Every time you sip water → **feel gratitude**
- Every time you step outside → **feel freedom**
- Every time you light a candle → **feel clarity**

69

PART 13

HOW TO GENERATE EMOTIONS ON-DEMAND

Over time, these become powerful emotional shortcuts.
They train your subconscious to shift instantly into magnetic frequencies.

✧ Don't wait. Create the emotion first.

The biggest block to manifestation is waiting.
Waiting to feel good after something happens.
Flip the script.
Create the emotion now — and become a match before the reality arrives. You're not faking. You're training your system to receive.

🔑 Key Takeaways:

- Emotion is not passive — it's a muscle you can build
- Use memory, body, and senses to activate feelings now
- Anchor emotions to daily rituals and objects
- Don't wait for life to change — change how you feel first
- Magnetic energy begins with emotional self-mastery

"The secret of change is to focus all of your energy not on fighting the old, but on building the new."
— Dan Millman

LETTING GO OF NEEDINESS

How Detachment Multiplies Your Attraction Power

One of the most paradoxical truths of manifestation is this:
The more you need push it away The more you can let go,
Neediness is a signal of lack.
It tells the universe: "I don't have this — and I'm afraid I won't."

That frequency is low, closed, and full of resistance.
Let's explore why letting go is not about giving up, but about trusting more deeply.

◇ Neediness blocks your energy field.

When you're attached to an outcome, you unconsciously:

- Obsess over timing
- Question every sign
- Doubt your worth
- Compare yourself to others
- Send mixed signals into the field

This frantic energy doesn't attract — it repels.
Because your vibration says, "I don't believe it's coming."
Detachment doesn't mean indifference.

LETTING GO OF NEEDINESS

It means inner stability regardless of what's happening outside.

◇ Desire is healthy. Obsession is not.

It's natural to want. Desire is the spark of creation.
But when desire turns into desperation, it activates fear —
and fear scrambles the signal.
Healthy desire says:

- "This would be beautiful."
- "I'm excited to receive it."
- "I trust the process."

Neediness says:

- "I need this or I'm not okay."
- "Why hasn't it happened yet?"
- "Something must be wrong with me."

The difference isn't in the words — it's in the frequency.

PART 14

LETTING GO OF
NEEDINESS

◇ Detachment is emotional freedom.

True power comes when you can say:
"I know what I want — and I'm okay even before it arrives."
This doesn't weaken your manifestation.
It makes it stronger — because it shifts you into a state of
having rather than lack.
Detachment means you're no longer begging. You're inviting.
Not chasing. Allowing.

◇ Act from vision, not from void.

When you act from a place of "trying to fill the hole,"
you attract more situations that reflect that hole.
But when you act from your vision already realized,
you become the version of you who already has what they
asked for.
That version is grounded. Open. Calm. Trusting.
And deeply magnetic.

LETTING GO OF NEEDINESS

◇ Practice surrender daily.

Letting go is not a one-time thing — it's a daily choice.
Try these practices to cultivate detachment:

- Write down your desire, feel it fully, then release it with gratitude
- Say: "This or something better is already on its way"
- Focus on how you want to feel, not just what you want to get
- Breathe into the unknown — and trust that the universe is orchestrating what you can't see yet

Surrender doesn't mean you stop caring.
It means you stop controlling.

LETTING GO OF NEEDINESS

🔑 Key Takeaways:

- Neediness is fear disguised as desire — and it creates resistance
- Detachment raises your frequency into trust, peace, and receiving
- You're most magnetic when you're aligned but not desperate
- Surrender is strength — it shows you're ready to receive
- Let go of "how" and "when" — focus on who you're becoming

"Only when you let go of the inner clinging, the need to control or possess, do you become free enough to receive all that life is offering you."
— Michael A. Singer

YOU ARE NOT YOUR THOUGHTS

The ego thrives on identification.

The ego survives by making you believe:
"I am my opinions."
"I am my fears."
"I am my past."
"I am this story."
But you are not the story.
You are the presence beneath the story — the consciousness watching it unfold.
Every time you observe a thought without attaching to it, your ego loses power... and your soul gains clarity.

◇ Reaction = unconsciousness.

When you believe every thought, you live in reaction mode:

- Someone criticizes you → **you collapse**
- A desire delays → **you panic**
- A fear appears → **you spiral**

But when you become the observer, you respond from conscious choice, not from wounded programming.
This shift alone can dissolve years of internal conflict.

PART 15

YOU ARE NOT YOUR THOUGHTS

◇ Meditation trains the witness.

The fastest way to access your true self is through stillness.
In meditation, you learn to:

- Notice thoughts without following them
- Sit with discomfort without resisting it
- Detach from identity and return to presence

You don't need to empty your mind — just watch it without judgment.
And in that watching, something powerful happens:
The watcher awakens.

◇ You have thoughts — but you are awareness.

Imagine standing at the edge of a river.
Thoughts are leaves floating by.
Most people jump in, grab every leaf, and drown in the current.
But you can stay on the shore.
You can watch without reacting.
You can choose which thoughts to follow — and which to release. That choice is your freedom.
That awareness is your true power.

PART 15
YOU ARE NOT YOUR THOUGHTS

🔑 **Key Takeaways:**

- You are not your thoughts — you are the observer of them
- The ego feeds on identification, but awareness breaks the loop
- Meditation teaches you to watch, not react
- Your freedom lies in choosing which thoughts to believe
- When you return to presence, you return to your power

"You are not your thoughts. You are the awareness behind them."
— Eckhart Tolle

BECOMING THE OBSERVER

Meditative Techniques to Reset Your Vibrational Field

When you stop identifying with your thoughts, you don't just find peace —
you unlock your power to reset your energy, shift your frequency, and attract from a place of stillness.
The observer is not passive.
It's the most powerful part of you — the one that can see without judgment, feel without drowning, and choose without reacting.
Let's explore how to activate the observer within you using simple meditative practices.

◇ Observation dissolves resistance.

Most people resist their thoughts and emotions:
"This shouldn't be happening."
"I shouldn't feel this way."
"I need to fix this now."
But resistance creates friction — and friction lowers your vibration.
Observation, on the other hand, creates space.
And space restores flow.
What you observe without resistance, you release.
What you accept without fear, you transform.

BECOMING THE OBSERVER

◇ The "watching mind" restores coherence.

When you shift from "I am thinking" to "I am watching thinking,"
your brainwaves begin to slow down.
Your nervous system calms.
Your field becomes coherent.
In this state:

- Your heart and brain synchronize
- Your thoughts lose emotional charge
- Your energetic signal becomes stable and clear

This is the ideal state for attraction — calm, coherent, and receptive.

◇ Simple practice: 5-minute observer meditation

1. Sit comfortably. Close your eyes.
2. Bring attention to your breath — don't control it, just notice.
3. Let thoughts arise.
4. With each thought, silently say:
5. "A thought is arising."
6. "I am not the thought. I am the one who sees it."
7. Watch the thought drift away, like a cloud in the sky.
8. Return to the breath. Repeat.

BECOMING THE OBSERVER

Do this for 5 minutes daily.
Even a short practice reconnects you with the real you.

◇ Use your day as a meditation.

You don't need to sit in silence to be the observer.
You can practice throughout the day:

- When you feel triggered: "Interesting. I notice tension."
- When a craving arises: "This is just a sensation passing through."
- When judgment appears: "There's a thought. Not the truth."

This doesn't make you cold or detached.
It makes you aware — and awareness brings choice.

◇ Let silence reset your signal.

Silence isn't empty. It's full of information.
Spend at least 10 minutes a day in stillness:

- No phone
- No input
- Just presence

BECOMING THE OBSERVER

In this silence, your mind settles.
Your field resets.
And your magnetism increases — because your energy is no longer scattered.

🔑 Key Takeaways:

- Becoming the observer dissolves resistance and restores flow
- Observation creates space — and space heals
- Short meditations rewire your brain and calm your field
- Presence in daily life is a form of silent mastery
- Silence sharpens your vibration and makes you magnetic

"Step back and watch your own mind. You will see the drama, the stories, the noise — and you will realize: none of it is you."
— Mooji

CO-CREATION WITH THE UNIVERSE

Aligning with Divine Timing and Intuitive Guidance

You are not manifesting alone.
There is a greater intelligence — call it the Universe, Source, Life, or God — that is always responding to your energy.
You are not here to control everything.
You are here to co-create.
When you shift from force to partnership, life becomes less about pushing... and more about listening, flowing, and allowing.

✧ You are part of something greater.

The same force that grows trees, spins galaxies, and beats your heart —
is also guiding the unfolding of your life.
You are not separate from the field.
You are a unique expression of it.
This means:

- You don't have to "figure it all out"
- You are allowed to be supported
- The answers you seek are already within reach

When you align your vibration with trust and openness, the Universe meets you halfway.

PART 17

CO-CREATION WITH THE UNIVERSE

✧ Intuition is divine GPS.

Your intuitive nudges are not random.
They are messages from the field — showing you the next right step, the hidden insight, the invisible opportunity.
But you can't hear them when your mind is loud.
To receive guidance, you must:

- Quiet the noise
- Pay attention to subtle pulls
- Act on inspiration, even without logic
- Trust the "yes" and "no" inside your body

Co-creation begins when you stop doubting your deeper knowing.

✧ Divine timing is not delay — it's alignment.

When something doesn't arrive on your schedule, don't assume it's not working.
Assume it's being orchestrated in ways you can't yet see.
Delays often mean:

- You're being protected
- You're being refined
- Something better is being prepared

CO-CREATION WITH THE UNIVERSE

The Universe is always on time — just not always on your time. Patience isn't waiting.
It's trusting in movement you cannot yet measure.

◇ Co-creation requires surrender and participation.

It's not enough to just visualize.
And it's not about hustling either.
It's about:

- Feeling the desire
- Aligning your vibration
- Taking inspired action
- Letting go of attachment
- Listening for the next signal

You are both initiator and receiver.
Both creator and listener.
This balance is the dance of manifestation.

CO-CREATION WITH THE UNIVERSE

✧ Signs and synchronicities are real.

Repeating numbers, chance meetings, sudden insights —
these are winks from the Universe.
When you notice them, celebrate.
They are confirmations that:
"Your energy is aligned. Keep going."
The more you acknowledge them, the more they appear —
because your field is now tuned to guidance, not doubt.

🔑 Key Takeaways:

- You are not manifesting alone — you are co-creating with a living intelligence
- Intuition is your inner compass, always guiding
- Divine timing ensures right outcomes at the right moment
- Co-creation is a balance of aligned action and deep surrender
- The Universe speaks in signs, symbols, and synchronicity — if you're willing to listen

"You are the universe expressing itself as a human for a little while."
— Eckhart Tolle

PART 18

KARMA, DHARMA AND THE LAW OF ATTRACTION

Why Not Everything You Want Is What You Truly Need

Sometimes you don't get what you want —
and it's not because the Law of Attraction "isn't working."
It's because something deeper is unfolding: your karmic path
and your soul's evolution.
This chapter explores the intersection between your desires,
your life purpose, and the unseen blueprint your soul carries
into this life.

◇ Karma is energy in motion.

Karma is not punishment.
It's the energetic consequence of choices made — in this life
or others.
Every thought, word, and action carries a frequency. That
frequency ripples out... and eventually returns.
Karma is about balance, learning, and growth.
Sometimes, you may attract an experience not because you
"wanted" it —
but because your soul needs it to complete a cycle or learn a
key lesson.

KARMA, DHARMA AND THE LAW OF ATTRACTION

◇ Dharma is your soul's path.

Dharma is your true purpose — the role your soul came here to embody.
It's the intersection of:

- **What you love**
- **What you're gifted at**
- **What serves others**
- **What elevates your spirit**

When you align with your dharma, you don't just manifest faster —
you manifest in harmony with your higher self.
Your desires stop being ego-driven, and start being soul-guided.

◇ The Universe doesn't respond to ego — it responds to alignment.

Sometimes, what you want is rooted in fear, image, or unworthiness:
"I want success so I feel valuable."
"I want love so I feel complete."

KARMA, DHARMA AND THE LAW OF ATTRACTION

But your higher self won't support manifestations that reinforce your wounds.
It will delay, redirect, or dismantle anything that pulls you out of alignment.
You don't attract what flatters the ego.
You attract what awakens the soul.

◇ **Pain can be part of the path.**

Yes, the Law of Attraction is real.
But so is contrast, challenge, and refinement.
Sometimes the "negative" experience is actually a course correction:

- A breakup that leads to self-love
- A failure that activates your purpose
- A delay that develops your intuition

These moments aren't proof that manifestation is broken.
They're proof that your soul is growing — and that something better is being born.

PART 18

KARMA, DHARMA AND THE LAW OF ATTRACTION

◇ **Surrender to the higher plan.**

You're allowed to desire. You're allowed to create.
But always hold your desires with open hands.
Say:
"This... or something better, aligned with my highest good."
"I trust the unseen wisdom guiding my life."
This isn't giving up control.
It's partnering with the part of you that sees further than
your mind ever could.

🔑 **Key Takeaways:**

- Karma is not punishment — it's energetic balance
- Dharma is your soul's unique path of expression and purpose
- The Universe favors alignment over ego
- Not all desires serve your evolution — and that's okay
- When you surrender to the higher plan, you magnetize what's truly meant for you

"Your karma is not in what is happening to you.
Your karma is in the way you respond to it."
— Sadhguru

THE MORNING MIND RITUAL

A Step-by-Step Daily Practice to Align Thought, Emotion, and Vibration

Manifestation isn't something you do once.
It's a daily calibration — a moment-to-moment choice to think, feel, and act from your highest self.
The most powerful way to shift your reality is to start each day with intention, clarity, and alignment.
This chapter gives you a simple but potent Morning Mind Ritual to activate your magnetic field — in under 20 minutes.

◇ Why morning matters

The first moments after waking are when your brain is in theta and alpha waves — highly receptive and programmable.
This is when your subconscious is most open.
It's your chance to set the energetic tone for your entire day.
Skip this, and your mind is hijacked by notifications, stress, or autopilot thinking.
But if you train your focus early, you create a day that flows with you, not against you.

THE MORNING MIND RITUAL

◇ The Morning Mind Ritual (10–20 min)

Step 1: Centering Breath (1–2 min)

- Sit comfortably
- Inhale through the nose for 4 seconds
- Hold for 4
- Exhale slowly for 6
- Repeat 5–6 cycles
- Feel your body arrive in the present

Step 2: Future-Self Visualization (3–5 min)

- Close your eyes
- See yourself living your ideal life
- Use all senses: What do you feel, hear, touch, say?
- Embody the emotion of already having it
- Smile gently as if it were already real

Step 3: Identity Affirmations (2–3 min)

Speak or write:

- "I am aligned with my highest timeline."
- "I allow success to flow to me today."
- "My thoughts create. My energy leads. I trust the process."
- Repeat each affirmation 3–5 times, with feeling.

THE MORNING MIND RITUAL

Step 4: Embodied Intention (2 min)
Stand up. Stretch. Breathe.
Say aloud or write:

"Today, I choose to show up as..." [confident / present / open / free]

Feel it in your posture and movement.

Optional Step 5: Quick Journaling (3–5 min)

Write down:

- One thing I'm grateful for
- One thing I'm calling in
- One thing I'm ready to release

◇ Make it your own.

You don't need to follow this perfectly.
Customize it based on your time, mood, and needs.
The key is consistency.
Even five minutes of conscious creation in the morning is better than hours of unconscious reaction.
This ritual is how you become the cause of your day — not its effect.

THE MORNING MIND RITUAL

🔑 Key Takeaways:

- Your morning state sets your vibration for the entire day
- The subconscious is most receptive right after waking
- Breath, vision, affirmation, and intention align your field
- A simple daily ritual reprograms your identity
- Manifestation begins with how you show up — not what you chase

"How you wake up each day and your morning routine (or lack thereof) dramatically affects your levels of success in every single area of your life."
— Hal Elrod

JOURNALING FOR MANIFESTATION

How Writing Reprograms Your Reality

Your thoughts shape your reality —
but when you write them down, you give them form, focus, and frequency.
Journaling isn't just self-reflection.
It's a powerful manifestation technology: it programs your subconscious, clarifies your desires, and reinforces the identity of the version of you that already has what you want.
In this chapter, you'll learn how to use journaling as a daily magnetic tool.

◇ Writing = Embodied Thought

When you write something down:

- You focus your mind
- You amplify your intention
- You ground your desire into the physical world

This turns vague wishes into conscious commands.
Your journal becomes a sacred space where your inner world becomes a blueprint for your outer reality.

PART 20

JOURNALING FOR MANIFESTATION

◇ What you write, you wire.

Neuroscience shows that writing creates deeper neural connections than thinking alone.
This means that what you repeatedly write, especially with emotion, becomes more believable to the subconscious. Every written affirmation, intention, and visualization helps build a new default setting in your brain — and in your energy field.

◇ Journaling Techniques for Manifestation

1. Scripting the Future (5–10 min)
Write as if your desired reality has already happened.

Example:
"I'm waking up in my new apartment overlooking the sea. I feel peaceful, abundant, and so proud of myself for making this shift."
Use details, emotions, and sensory language.
2. Gratitude in Advance (3–5 min)
List things you're grateful for before they arrive.
Example:

- "Thank you for the aligned clients."
- "Thank you for the loving partnership."
- "Thank you for the clarity in my purpose."

JOURNALING FOR MANIFESTATION

This tells your subconscious: "It's already done."

3. Identity Statements (daily)
Write:
- "I am..."
- "I choose..."
- "I feel..."
- Example:
- "I am safe to receive more."
- "I choose to speak my truth."
- "I feel aligned with abundance."

4. Belief Upgrade
Write down an old belief, then replace it with a new one.
Example:
Old: "Money is hard to keep."
New: "Money flows to me and stays with love."

◇ **Make it sacred.**

- Use a notebook that feels special
- Journal at the same time each day (ideally morning or evening)
- Light a candle, play soft music, or create a calming space
- Keep your writing private and judgment-free

The more sacred the space feels, the more powerful the shift becomes.

JOURNALING FOR MANIFESTATION

🔑 Key Takeaways:

- Writing turns mental energy into physical reality
- Journaling reprograms the subconscious faster than thought alone
- Scripting, gratitude, and identity work align your vibration
- A daily writing ritual becomes a magnet for clarity and change
- Your journal is not just a tool — it's a portal to your future self

Note: If you'd like to experience guided journaling in action, you can try the platform my company created: www.devamastery.com

"Writing is medicine. It is an appropriate antidote to injury. It is an appropriate companion for any difficult change."
— Julia Cameron

THE 3X33, 5X55, AND SCRIPTING METHODS

Powerful Manifestation Exercises That Rewire Your Mind

Manifestation isn't just about what you think once.
It's about what you repeat consistently, with emotion and intention.
The following journaling techniques use repetition, emotion, and focused energy to impress new beliefs into your subconscious — and send a clear signal into the quantum field.
These tools are simple but powerful. Use them with devotion, not desperation.

◇ The 3x33 Method

How it works:

- Choose one affirmation or intention
- Write it 33 times a day, for 3 days in a row

Example:
"I am now aligned with financial freedom."
Why it works:
Repetition + focused attention + short time span = deep subconscious imprint.

THE 3X33, 5X55, AND SCRIPTING METHODS

Tips:
- Keep your affirmation short, believable, and emotionally charged
- Don't rush — feel each repetition
- After you finish, sit for 2 minutes and visualize the result

◇ The 5x55 Method

How it works:

- Choose one specific intention
- Write it 55 times a day, for 5 days in a row

Example:
"I am so grateful I now attract loving, supportive relationships."

Why it works:
This technique intensifies repetition and emotional energy over a longer window, pushing through resistance and mental clutter.

Tips:

- Do it when you have space — it takes 20–30 minutes
- Stay present: it's not about speed, it's about energy
- Use music or breath to stay grounded during the process

THE 3X33, 5X55, AND SCRIPTING METHODS

◇ Scripting Method

How it works:

- Write a journal entry describing your dream life or specific manifestation
- Use past tense or present perfect, as if it already happened
- Include feelings, details, and sensory descriptions

Example:
"Today I signed the contract for my dream client. I'm so proud of how aligned it felt. The whole process was smooth and joyful. I celebrated with a walk by the river and a quiet moment of gratitude."

Why it works:
Your subconscious processes imagery and feeling more powerfully than logic. Writing a scene with detail tricks the mind into believing it's real — and begins aligning your vibration to that frequency.
Tips:

- Write in a relaxed emotional state
- Read it aloud after writing
- Revisit your favorite scripts often and refine them

THE 3X33, 5X55, AND SCRIPTING METHODS

✧ Which one should you use?

- Short on time? Use 3x33
- Want a deep rewire? Use 5x55
- Love creativity and feeling? Use scripting
- Want the strongest shift? Combine them

You can alternate techniques or stick with one until you see results.
The method is less important than the emotion, presence, and belief behind it.

🔑 Key Takeaways:

- Repetition imprints new beliefs into the subconscious
- The 3x33 and 5x55 methods use structure to intensify intention
- Scripting uses imagination and feeling to align your frequency
- The power lies not in the words, but in your emotional energy
- Consistency and embodiment create real energetic change

"I choose to make the rest of my life the best of my life.
Repetition is the key to change."
— Louise Hay

THE ROLE OF INSPIRED ACTION

Trusting the Signs, Acting Without Fear

Manifestation is not just about thinking and feeling —
it's also about doing.
But not just any action.
Inspired action is movement that comes from alignment,
clarity, and intuition — not from fear, pressure, or
desperation.
This chapter will show you how to recognize inspired action,
trust it, and use it to build a bridge between your inner vision
and outer reality.

◇ Action is part of the vibration.

Many people believe they should "just trust the universe and
wait."
But waiting without action often becomes passive resistance.
Manifestation is a co-creative dance:
You align your frequency — and then follow the path that
appears.
Inspired action is not forced.

PART 22

THE ROLE OF INSPIRED ACTION

It feels like:

- A sudden idea that excites you
- A message you feel called to send
- A step that feels bold but aligned
- A small move that feels meaningful

It's the nudge that whispers, "Go now."

⬦ Fear-based action vs. inspired action

Fear-based action:

- Comes from panic or urgency
- Feels heavy, exhausting
- Lacks joy and clarity
- Is driven by "I have to" energy

Inspired action:

- Comes from calm inner knowing
- Feels light, exciting, or meaningful
- Often bypasses logic — but feels right
- Is driven by purpose, not pressure

Learn to recognize the quality of the energy behind your decisions.

THE ROLE OF INSPIRED ACTION

◇ The signs appear after alignment.

You won't always know the whole path.
But when your vibration is aligned, the next step becomes clear.
Examples:

- A person mentions a resource you needed
- A sudden opportunity shows up
- You feel pulled toward a certain place or message

These aren't random — they're invitations.
Your job is to say yes to them — even if they don't fully "make sense" yet.

◇ Don't wait for certainty. Move with clarity.

You rarely get the full roadmap.
You get a direction. A pull. A whisper.
And when you act on it —
the universe responds with more clarity.
Staying stuck because you're unsure is how dreams dissolve.
Progress comes from trusting the next step, not seeing the whole staircase.

PART 22

THE ROLE OF INSPIRED ACTION

◇ **Small steps shift big timelines.**

Inspired action doesn't mean quitting your job overnight or moving to another country tomorrow.
It can be:

- Sending one email
- Signing up for a class
- Decluttering your space
- Sharing your idea
- Saying "no" to something out of alignment

The key is momentum.
Aligned movement activates your field.

THE ROLE OF INSPIRED ACTION

🔑 Key Takeaways:

- Action grounded in alignment amplifies manifestation
- Inspired action feels expansive, not forced
- Don't wait for perfect clarity — follow intuitive nudges
- The universe guides you through signs and feelings
- Small, bold steps open new realities — one choice at a time

"You are not here to prove anything to anyone. You are here to align with who you really are, and then move from that inspired place."
— Abraham Hicks

HOW TO HANDLE DELAYS AND SETBACKS

Staying Magnetic Even When It Seems "Nothing's Happening"

Manifestation doesn't always look the way you expect.
Sometimes things seem slow, blocked, or even going backwards.
But here's the truth:
Just because you don't see progress, doesn't mean nothing is shifting.
Delays and setbacks are not signs of failure — they are invitations to deepen your trust, recalibrate your energy, and release hidden resistance.
Let's explore how to stay aligned, even in the waiting.

◇ The unseen is still active.

Like seeds under the soil, your desires may be growing where you can't see.
Roots are forming. Energy is moving. Timelines are adjusting.
Just because results are not visible, doesn't mean they're not real.
Your job is not to force the outcome —
but to maintain the frequency of already having it.

HOW TO HANDLE DELAYS AND SETBACKS

◇ Resistance often peaks before the shift.

Many people feel discouraged right before a breakthrough.
Why?
Because the old identity is being challenged.
The ego is losing grip.
And the nervous system is being rewired.
This can feel like:

- Doubt
- Fatigue
- Impatience
- Chaos

But it's often a sign that something is about to shift — if you stay the course.

◇ Don't attach to the form or timing.

Your manifestation may arrive:

- Through a different path than expected
- At a different time
- In a better version than you imagined

HOW TO HANDLE DELAYS AND SETBACKS

Attachment to how and when creates friction.
Letting go allows flow.
Repeat to yourself:
"This or something better is already aligning in divine timing."

◇ Use setbacks as recalibration points.

Instead of asking,
"Why is this happening to me?"
ask,
"What is this trying to show me?"
Often, delays reveal:

- A belief that needs clearing
- A boundary that needs strengthening
- A pattern that's ready to be released

Every "setback" is feedback — and growth is the reward.

PART 23

HOW TO HANDLE DELAYS
AND SETBACKS

◇ Return to alignment — no matter what.

Your power is not in the outcome.
Your power is in your state.
When things feel stuck:

- **Breathe**
- **Journal**
- **Visualize**
- **Move your body**
- **Reconnect with gratitude**
- **Remind yourself who you're becoming**

You don't have to be perfect — just consistent.

🔑 Key Takeaways:

- Delays are often part of alignment, not signs of failure
- The unseen world may be shifting in your favor
- Resistance can peak just before transformation
- Let go of "how" and "when" — focus on being the version who receives
- Return to alignment every day, no matter what the outside looks like

HOW TO HANDLE DELAYS AND SETBACKS

"Above all, trust in the slow work of God. We are quite naturally impatient in everything to reach the end without delay. We should like to skip the intermediate stages. But growth is by stages... and it is the law of all progress that it is made by passing through some stages of instability — and that it may take a very long time."
— Pierre Teilhard de Chardin

PART 24

SIGNS, SYNCHRONICITIES, AND FEEDBACK LOOPS

Interpreting the Universe's Response

The universe is not silent.
It is constantly speaking to you — **through signs, symbols, people, numbers, dreams, emotions, and chance encounters.**
But to receive these messages, you must learn to notice, interpret, and respond.
This chapter teaches you how to recognize synchronicities as real-time feedback from the field — and how to use them to stay in alignment.

◇ Signs are reflections of your frequency.

Every moment, the outer world mirrors your inner vibration. The stronger your alignment, the more visible the reflections.
Signs can come as:

- Repeating numbers (11:11, 222, 777)
- Animal encounters or symbols
- Songs with perfect lyrics
- Random people saying the exact thing you needed
- Objects, ads, or images that speak directly to your situation

SIGNS, SYNCHRONICITIES, AND FEEDBACK LOOPS

These are not coincidences — they are confirmation.
"Your signal has been received. Keep going."

◇ Synchronicity = alignment in motion.

When you begin to see patterns and connections that seem "too perfect,"
you're experiencing synchronicity — the universe arranging events to support your path.
This means:

- You're on the right track
- Your vibration is strong and clear
- Your intention is being echoed in the field

The more you acknowledge synchronicities, the more they multiply.
Gratitude = amplification.

SIGNS, SYNCHRONICITIES, AND FEEDBACK LOOPS

◇ Feedback loops reveal your current signal.

What's showing up in your reality — right now — is the best indicator of your dominant frequency.
If you're seeing:

- Clarity, ease, joy → **you're aligned**
- Confusion, tension, resistance → **your signal may be mixed or fear-based**

Don't judge yourself.
Simply adjust your state, not the circumstances.
Your outer reality is a delayed mirror of your inner reality.

◇ Ask and watch.

You can invite the universe to speak more clearly.
Try saying:

- "Show me a clear sign I'm aligned."
- "Give me a symbol today that confirms I'm supported."
- "Reveal what I need to know about this decision."

SIGNS, SYNCHRONICITIES, AND FEEDBACK LOOPS

Then let go — and stay open.
The sign may come in a form you don't expect.
Stay receptive, curious, and grounded.

◇ **Intuition + signs = inner and outer guidance.**

Signs are external.
Intuition is internal.
Together, they form a powerful guidance system.
When a sign appears and your body lights up with a "yes" — trust it.
When a sign feels off, confusing, or forced — pause and listen deeper.
You are not meant to chase signs.
You are meant to live so aligned that signs naturally surround you.

SIGNS, SYNCHRONICITIES, AND FEEDBACK LOOPS

🔑 Key Takeaways:

- Signs and synchronicities are real-time feedback from the universe
- The outer world mirrors your inner vibration
- Gratitude for signs strengthens the signal
- You can ask for confirmation — and trust how it comes
- Signs are invitations, not instructions — your intuition is the final guide

"Coincidences are not accidents but signals from the universe which can guide us toward our true destiny."
— Deepak Chopra

LIVING AS A MAGNET, NOT A BEGGAR

Embodying Your New Frequency

The ultimate goal is not just to "manifest" things.
It's to become someone who naturally attracts what aligns —
without effort, without desperation, without pretending.
This chapter is about the final shift:
from wanting to being,
from asking to radiating,
from chasing to receiving.

◇ Stop begging the universe. Start becoming the universe.

You don't have to plead, push, or prove.
You are not a beggar hoping to be chosen.
You are a magnet — when you choose to align.
When you live in the energy of already having, already trusting, already knowing...
reality bends to reflect that.

PART 25

LIVING AS A MAGNET, NOT A BEGGAR

✧ Identity is the core of attraction.

Your results are shaped by who you believe you are.
If you see yourself as:

- Struggling → **you attract struggle**
- Lacking → **you attract lack**
- Powerful → **you attract opportunity**
- Whole → **you attract love**

The most magnetic people don't just say affirmations —
they embody the version of themselves who already lives the
life they desire.
That identity radiates clarity, ease, and quiet power.

✧ Walk like it's done.

This doesn't mean faking.
It means feeling first, then choosing actions that reflect that
state.
Ask yourself daily:

- How would I move if I already had this?
- How would I speak? Dress? Decide?
- What would I stop tolerating?
- What would I celebrate more?

LIVING AS A MAGNET, NOT A BEGGAR

The more you align with this version — emotionally, mentally, physically —
the more your field stabilizes into attraction mode.

◇ Confidence is coherence.

True magnetism isn't loud or flashy.
It's quiet, calm, grounded.
It's the vibration of someone who doesn't need to prove —
because they already know.
Confidence is not arrogance.
It's energetic coherence:
"I am who I say I am."
"I live in the energy of what I want — now."

◇ Attraction becomes your nature.

At this point, manifestation is no longer a technique.
It's a byproduct of your frequency.
You don't try to attract.
You simply are magnetic — because your mind, body, and soul are in harmony.
You've moved from doing... to being.
From searching... to shining.
From lack... to embodiment.
And the world begins to respond — effortlessly.

LIVING AS A MAGNET, NOT A BEGGAR

🔑 Key Takeaways:

- You are not here to chase — you're here to radiate
- Who you believe you are defines what you receive
- Live as if it's done — from energy, not ego
- Magnetism is calm, confident, and embodied
- Manifestation becomes natural when your identity and frequency align

"You were born with wings, why prefer to crawl through life?"
— Rumi

THE JOURNEY OF EXPANSION

There Is Always More: Joy, Peace, and Purpose

Manifestation is not the end — it's the beginning.
Once you receive what you asked for, a deeper truth
emerges:
You didn't want the thing.
You wanted the feeling
And that feeling — joy, peace, freedom, love — was available
to you all along.
This chapter is about continuing the journey beyond goals,
beyond outcomes, into a life of continuous expansion.

◇ Desire is sacred — and endless.

You are not meant to be static.
Your soul craves growth, discovery, creativity.
Every fulfilled desire leads to a new edge, a new level of
becoming.
And that's beautiful.
Not because you're incomplete — but because you are
infinite.
Expansion is not greed.
It's the nature of life itself.

THE JOURNEY OF EXPANSION

◇ Peace is not the absence of desire — it's non-attachment to outcome.

You can want more while still feeling whole.
You can set big visions without being frantic.
This is the dance of expansion:

- Wanting from love, not lack
- Creating from joy, not fear
- Exploring from fullness, not emptiness

When you live this way, every step forward is a celebration — not a chase.

◇ Give what you've received.

Manifestation becomes meaningful when you share the overflow.

- If you've found abundance, help others rise.
- If you've found peace, become a presence of calm.
- If you've found purpose, teach by example.

Service multiplies your vibration.
What you give freely returns — not just in form, but in fulfillment.

THE JOURNEY OF EXPANSION

◇ Keep growing your edge.

Never stop asking:

- Who am I becoming now?
- What feels exciting, true, and expansive?
- Where is my soul calling me next?

Don't get stuck in yesterday's dream.
You are allowed to change, evolve, and want more.
Not because you're broken — but because you're becoming.

◇ Let joy be your new compass.

In the beginning, you may have used pain to motivate change.
But now, let joy lead the way.
Follow what feels light, expansive, and alive.
This is your soul's language — and it always leads to more of who you really are.

THE JOURNEY OF EXPANSION

🔑 **Key Takeaways:**

- Fulfillment is found in the feeling, not the thing
- Expansion is natural — it's how the soul expresses itself
- Peace comes from non-attachment, not passivity
- What you give from overflow returns multiplied
- Let joy and curiosity lead your next chapter

"You never get it done, and you can't get it wrong. That's the deliciousness of your eternal becoming. You are on the leading edge of thought, constantly expanding. Each new desire, each new contrast, each new moment — it all adds to the never-ending unfolding of who you really are. And the Universe is responding to every part of that with precision and love."
— Abraham Hicks

PROTECT YOUR DREAM

Guard It Like a Flame in the Wind

Your dream is sacred.
It's a frequency, a vision, a seed of a future reality that only you can feel — at first.
But because it is fragile in the beginning, it must be protected, not exposed.

Until it becomes strong enough to stand on its own, your dream needs silence, focus, and devotion — not approval, not debate, not explanation.

◇ Talking too soon can weaken your energy.

Sharing your vision too early — especially with people who don't understand manifestation — often leads to:

- Doubt
- Unwanted opinions
- Rational "advice" that kills inspiration
- Energy leaks and second-guessing

Your dream is not a democracy.
It doesn't need validation.
It needs commitment.

PROTECT YOUR DREAM

◇ Energy moves where attention flows.

Every time you speak of your dream, you're directing energy
to it. If you speak with certainty, you amplify the vibration.
If you speak with fear, or around people who don't believe,
you distort it.

Be selective with your words.
Be protective of your frequency.

Silence isn't secrecy — it's sovereignty.

◇ Let your results speak first.

In the early stages, your dream lives inside of you.
Let it grow roots before asking others to water it.

You don't need to convince.
You don't need to perform.

When your dream begins to manifest — when people see the
change, feel your glow, witness the alignment —
you won't need to explain.
They'll ask.

Let your energy become the message.
Let your reality become the proof.

PROTECT YOUR DREAM

✧ Sacred privacy builds magnetic strength.

Create a ritual around your vision:

- **Write it**
- **Feel it**
- **Speak it to the Universe — not the crowd**
- **Act on it in private**
- **Protect it like it's alive (because it is)**

In silence, your dream gathers power.
In action, it gains momentum.
In time, it becomes unshakable.

🔑 Key Takeaways:

- Not everyone is meant to understand your dream
- Speaking too soon can invite doubt and distort your frequency
- Silence protects energy and allows clarity to build
- Results are the most magnetic proof — let them come first
- Treat your dream as sacred, and it will become undeniable

PROTECT YOUR DREAM

"Your imagination is a preview of life's coming attractions, but don't expect everyone to see it. When God puts a vision in your heart, it wasn't a conference call. It was a personal revelation. That means not everybody will understand it — and they don't have to. Protect your dream. Feed it. Water it. Guard it from those who can't see what you see, until the dream is strong enough to walk on its own."

— Steve Harvey

GRATITUDE: THE HIGHEST FREQUENCY

The Most Powerful Emotion of All

There are many emotions on the vibrational spectrum. Joy, love, peace, confidence, inspiration — each one holds power.
But there is one that seems to open every door, dissolve resistance, and instantly shift your energy field:
Gratitude.

Gratitude is pure receptivity.
It's the energetic signal that says,

"I already have. I already am. And I welcome more."

In moments of fear, anxiety, or doubt, no emotion cuts through the noise more effectively than gratitude.

PART 28

GRATITUDE: THE
HIGHEST FREQUENCY

✧ Why gratitude is stronger than fear

Most people try to overcome fear by "fixing" something on
the outside.
But fear doesn't leave because life gets perfect — it leaves
when your energy becomes **undeniably safe.**

That's what gratitude does.
It tells your nervous system:

"There is goodness here. I'm not in danger."

When you embody that, you stop sending signals of lack, and
you start radiating **magnetic coherence.**

✧ Gratitude overrides the lower mind

The ego always wants more.
It sees what's missing. It compares. It complains.

Gratitude sees what's present. It appreciates. It expands.
And in doing so, it moves you from contraction to expansion,
from fear to flow.

You don't need the perfect life to feel grateful.
You just need to notice what's already true.

131

GRATITUDE: THE HIGHEST FREQUENCY

◇ A daily dose of power

Make gratitude a ritual, not a reaction.

Each day, ask yourself:

- What am I genuinely thankful for right now?
- What do I take for granted that is actually a gift?
- What small beauty did I almost miss today?

Then write it.
Feel it.
Let it shift your state — even if only for a few seconds.

Those seconds matter. They compound.
They train your brain to focus on abundance, not absence.

◇ Gratitude is not passive. It's generative.

It's not about being polite or "positive."
It's about activating the frequency of wholeness — the vibration where new realities emerge.

Gratitude doesn't just make you feel good.
It makes you magnetic.

PART 28

GRATITUDE: THE HIGHEST FREQUENCY

🔑 **Key Takeaways:**

- Among all emotions, gratitude is one of the highest frequencies
- It dissolves fear, rewires the brain, and opens your field
- Gratitude is a conscious practice — not a reaction to perfection
- It turns your focus from what's lacking to what's already working
- The more you feel it, the more you attract situations that match it

"Be thankful for what you have; you'll end up having more. If you concentrate on what you don't have, you will never, ever have enough."
— Oprah Winfrey

FINAL MESSAGE

Your Life Is Your Most Powerful Creation

You've reached the end of this book —
but the real journey is just beginning.
Because now, you're not just reading about the Law of
Attraction...
You understand it, feel it, and embody it.
And that changes everything.

✧ You are not a passive observer of life.

You are a creator, a vibrational being, a conscious force of
nature.
You carry within you the power to shape timelines, shift
energy, and call in realities aligned with your highest truth.
Your thoughts matter.
Your emotions speak.
Your frequency leads.

✧ It's not about perfection. It's about presence.

You don't need to be high-vibe all the time.
You don't need to manifest flawlessly.
You simply need to return — again and again —

PART 29

FINAL MESSAGE

to the version of you who remembers:

- "I am safe."
- "I am powerful."
- "I am the signal."
- "I am already enough."

Even five minutes of presence can change the entire day.
One conscious breath can realign your field.
One choice made from truth can shift your destiny.

◇ Let your life become the proof.

You don't need to convince anyone.
You don't need to explain this work.
Just live it.
Let your energy speak louder than your words.
Let your peace be louder than your hustle.
Let your joy become your impact.
Your life — as it evolves — will inspire others to remember
who they are.
That's the true ripple effect of manifestation.

FINAL MESSAGE

✧ From this point forward...

- Be intentional with your thoughts.
- Be loving with your emotions.
- Be clear with your desires.
- Be bold with your actions.
- Be anchored in your truth.

And always remember:
You are not here to beg for your dreams.
You are here to become them.

With love,
Alberto

"The greatest danger for most of us is not that our aim is too high and we miss it, but that it is too low and we reach it. I am still learning."
— Michelangelo

Made in United States
Cleveland, OH
18 July 2025

18652438R10079